. . . only the trying . . .

Only the trying!
— Love
Meme

. . . only the trying . . .

by

David J. Thomas

Brunswick

"Stopping by Splices on a Typical Evening," a parody of the Robert Frost 1923 classic "Stopping by Woods on a Snowy Evening," has previously appeared in *English Journal* 73.1 (1984) and *Robert Frost Review* (Fall 1992).

Cover photo by James D. Thomas.

International Standard Book Number
1-55618-169-8

Library of Congress Catalog Card Number
98-70218

First Original Edition
Published in the United States of America
by

Brunswick Publishing Corporation
1386 Lawrenceville Plank Road
Lawrenceville, Virginia 23868
1-800-336-7154

For us, there is only the trying.
The rest is not our business.

— T. S. ELIOT
Four Quartets; "East Coker, II"

This book is dedicated to John W. Hattman, my mentor and friend.

Including "Jack" Hattman, those others responsible for inspiring, encouraging, and tolerating my creative writing are: A. Tracey Lallone, James D. Thomas, Paula J. Waller, and Walter R. Wieloh.

Table of Contents

abloom

March discovered daffodil buds
under the promise of silver snow
feeling into a cold unfolding
flickering between forgetting and not:
i witnessed the unuttered solitude
of a most powerful blooming
fluttering dream-light yellows
converting custom into conviction
blossoming back the past
blossoming back the year

advice

when in doubt,
write it out:
recompose yourself!

. . . and why . . .

. . . and why
   this wet, brown tree
   reaches tenaciously
   with cold, naked fingers
   toward the grey-paleness
   of early-evening
   in late-winter

. . . and why
   question the need
   to do so

baby dreams

her words were cribbed within a misty dream—
two fetal forms lying
tossed unsleeping memories
and
whispered high-blue hopes—
but only the night heard . . .

t h e

b a l l o o n

t r a n s l u c e n t

the   translucent   balloon

bu   r   s   t   s

the baby into

c

r

y

i

n

g

!

butter-fly

!

e   r   y

l   t   t   -   b

f   u

caught in the act

caught in the act
while lying with,
but not to, one another
in the twisted tangle
of your unmade bed
as the faint morning light
crept up
behind the yellowed shade
and slanted across the wall
opposite us

when, just then—
someone driving a truck
pulled into your driveway,
and the digital clock flashed 6:11,
6:11—and time for action:
fumbling for a lost tennis shoe,
i made a quick re-vision
of an earlier decision,
and finding only a black, spiked heel
beneath the clothes
puddled upon the floor
and no need to conceal our love,
i fell back into your warm embrace,
willing to be caught in the act

cheers

before coffee and after wine
are when my brain don't work so fine:
full of emptiness, geez-o-whiz—
not good, not bad, but only is;
the thunder comes and then the snow:
my push is pulled so coldly so;
smoothly fast it evaporates,
comes heavily behind my hates—
i must believe, or i must think:
i know i need another drink,
but if of grape or if of bean—
i'm not too sure of what (i mean)

Cipro-dream

after arising from my deathbed, i
Cipro-dream myself into awaking—
bleary eyes and cloudy mind tempted
by the breaking light; the promise
of grayness greets me drearily as i
stumble into the frigid kitchen, a
morning morgue, onto the cold
linoleum, my feet burnt into
numbness—cold soul, numb-dumb:
blindly, i finger-punch the on-
button of the anthracitic coffee maker,
prompting percolation prevarication:
my Mr. Coffee is a liar who boasts
of being a four-cupper, but even
filled past the silver band, he turns
water into coffee—a two-and-a-
quarter-cup miracle—and no more!

then, the revision of the earliest
decision: torn between the commitment
to day's other chores and the invitation
to revisitation of death's second-self,
i wonder inside silently, wearily:
could Jesus have done it 364 more
times in His final year, thirty-something
AD (AD?—Automatic Drip?—I smile)
suppositionally), and did anyone offer
Him coffee on that first Easter Sunday?

Courtney Love, you

crawled out onto stage from blackest
Hole, blond-white, like death on a
soda-cracker, leaning and yearning
toward the frenzied gestures of the
crowd: gyrations defiant, cacophonous
syncopation born from finger-fucking
your guitar; Madonna-Medusa tempting
dirt-made-flesh into beatific daughter
of grunge-father; the last synchroflash
revealing (smoke-enclouded) frazzle—
Stevie Nicks with a thumping hangover:
lips, forbidden-fruit-blossoms, spitting
bullets skyward into Nirvana, wish-
wanting whose suicide—if not his,
perhaps your own!?

David:
The Bubble-boy
(1971-1984)

defenseless against Goliath,
transplanted freshly
from the hands of God
to a sterile, vinyl womb—
immune to earthly pleasure—
nourished by your sister's essence,
born into captivity:
kissing and hugging barefaced
with your mother
fifteen days before dying;

triumphant against Goliath,
transferred again
by the hands of God
into a bronze, floral casket—
immune to earthly pain—
nurtured by your parents' courage,
died into freedom:
running and skipping barefooted
to your Father
fifteen days after aborning

days do not dissolve

days do not dissolve
the memories;
tears do not wash
them away,

yet both still come—
together, unannounced—
like careless whispers
disordering my dreams
and
stealing my time—

softly,

sadly

d

e

s

i

r

e

flaming away in formless flight
trembling a blue-green-yellow light
glimmer and glitter, flash and flare
soft liquid flutters into air
restless dancing: remembered fear
flicker-forgetting: nowhere near
shivering fingers melt and fade
flowering whisps of flatter made
sighing silently into smoke
withering wisdom it awoke

dream collusion

for the past several nights,
a whim has been cantering
across the plains of my mind,
victimizing my sleep.

the marauder gallops dustily
into the highlands—unapprehended!

your face yellows
on a wanted poster,
guilty of complicity!

dying agnostically

afraid to breathe again,
afraid to feel the pain again,
she stopped—forever:

her severed soul slid
into the black abyss of nothingness,

and like a butterfly with crumpled wings,
it edged its way—
up and fro and to and down
in broken rhythm—

forever

early impression-ist

and i remember,
little Manet,
as you Crayolaed iridescently
the beige hallway wall:
pushing and pulling your talent
in asymetrical configurations;
creatively, you urged the blandness
away from the boring canvas;
mistakenly, you urged
your mother's frowning countenance
away from her bread-baking;
your prolonged silence, no doubt,
had attracted her attention—

then, as the dampened rag,
saturated with Lestoil,
was thrust in your direction
and the command resounded,
your all-too-brief career
was being expunged
as you puddled to the floor
in histrionic protestation!

early reflection

the frozen, steamy boredom
     eyes in curious photograph
the bareness of my disordered dream—

it signals   my   isolation

it dissipates
   like fading stars of memory
      amidst smoke-rings swirling within:

as mirror echoes mirror,
     the sunlight encroaches
  upon my solitary patch of shadow
        and
  i blunder into the pain of another   d

                              a

                                   y

entelechy

something in me going on—
keeping me awake till dawn,
twisting wildly in my head,
squirming me around my bed,
chasing me throughout the night,
pushing me to mourning light—
something in me always cries;
something in me never dies!

frightmare

sleep, at night, goes away from me,
but then a pillow-wrestling thought
a waking dream of that to be—
comes upon me, though it ought not:

that vivid scene, as i can see,
twists my emotions in a knot;
it frightens fear so awfully
that i fear it cannot be fought

glistening

the shadows of golden things,
glimmers that the sunshine brings,
which adorn my daily dreams
glitter brightest, so it seems,

when grayish puffs reveal rays
which have hidden many days—
diamond-like and brightening,
glowing, golden, frightening

hangover dreams

dreams—
charcoal-grey shadows—
wavering in misty vagueness
warping and fading vestiges of
    past regrets
    daily fears
    future desires
hollow thoughts, twisting
lurking in the recesses
waiting for fulfillment:
    fleeting glimpses
    haunting faces—

apparitional promises

Hunh?!

O G I 2 C
U 8 1 T-V
B-4 A T-P
2 B A Q-T

in the distance

in the distance
through the sparkly shimmer
of the final sip
of my last drink,
your inviting visage is
erased and rephrased
by the elbowing, swaying crowd,

and, just then . . .

I recollect
a solitary patch
of daffodils
reaching yellowly skyward
through the snow—

promising today only

in response to "[your] response . . ."

i now visit alone, not grieving, in Wheeling,
    West Virginia,
but attempting to recollect my first visitation
with Itsy, Rico, Weasel, and Fred,
curious Catholic teens from Burgettstown,
    Pennsylvania,
years ago, down along the littered Ohio banks;
we hid behind the railroad cars,
not far from the raucous music of The Palace,
ready to relinquish our secret savings,
watching the back door—
    waiting, worrying, wondering.

we crept through the darkness
to Twenty-Third and Water streets
nearby Wheeling Spring Service
where the doors opened in early evening;
guarding our wallets, we men-boys
slid down the back alley to the whorehouse
and through the hymeneal door.

i do not clearly recall how it was then . . . .

but now the whorehouse, condemned again,
   is defunct—
dilapidated white-washed walls cradle shattered
   windows,
the plywood sheathing erected after the penetration:
spent condoms, shards of brown bottles, and
twisted cigarette butts punctuate the perimeter;
a frightened cat hunkers and scurries away
across the rusty springs, remnants of burnt mattresses,
(and I smile to myself at the potential pun).

but a few blocks away at the My Club,
on the hellish shore, they dry their wings still—
for nobody involved dares to commit suicide:
St. Vincent de Paul offers necessary rehabilitation,
   in time of need;
there are no accidental baptisms in the polluted river
   across from Bridgeport, Ohio.

James at the window

I

as you gazed dumbfoundedly,
clenched fists pocketed,
out of your parents' bedroom window,
out into the mystery of night,
your moist-eyed reflection—
angry with confusion: confused with anger—
shot back into the dimly-lit room
where your mother lay prone
upon her cold bed—the very bed
where you were conceived and suckled—
sobbing uncontrollably,
her face hidden in her wet hands,
her hands buried in the stained pillow—
her *crix de coeur* muffled;
where a strange man
who was your father
(but who couldn't be!)
who was supposed to be your mother's husband
stood half-drunken, half-frozen
intending nocturnal departure
through October-chilled rain,
he, himself, unable to understand:
inexplicable reasons, unvoiced words
fell, scatteringly, to the hardwood floor
like broken Tinker-Toy promises

II

outside the mirror-like pane of glass
near where you stood,
but invisible to most
of the bedroom's occupants,
two dusty-grey doves
nestled themselves,
beak-to-back and back-to-beak,
into resting position
beneath the drooping remainders
of the frost-bitten garden

Judas-eyes

your guilty eyes
reveal your lies
despite the words you say:

your guiltiness,
you must confess,
your eyes your lips betray

Lanie,

a lone wildflower,
grew basking in sunshine,
ecstatically radiant,
misplaced
on Main Hall steps
across from hacky-sack practice,
among friends and stray canines;

still—smiling, flourishing
even in dank shadows
of past doubts
and
despite ominous skies greying
(as in her eyes)
over future dreams:

summering, blooming,
living life care-freely . . .

until . . .

discontent fell,
frost-like,
and an all-too-early
winter stole—
abruptly!—
this precious wildflower
and left
only
a
cold
blanket of white.

last May

last May:
lonesome wondering,
but not lost

proven June:
invitation—inviting
aqua-marine twinkle;
bodies yearning
in direction
of each other,
of an us;
lasting love,
but not lost—
pushing, thrusting
into July:
through Dead love
into lost weekend—
alone crying,
naked cuddling—
two learning to(o)
be still,
still being . . .

together wandering,
but not lost—
may last

leaf dream

i dreamt a dream about a dream,
so strangely real—now—it does seem:
a brown leaf rustles in the wind,
it tells of someone who has sinned,
it blows across the meadows green,
it recalls nothing i have seen,
it tumbles, twists, and floats away,
it leaves its past in yesterday,
it throws itself against a tree,
it struggles, then, to become free:
a dream about me—so it seems;
i wonder if the brown leaf dreams . . .

leave-taking

with the importance of oaks,
we push slowly out
from sleepless-dreamless suspension
into a land of timorous shadows;
overwhelmed by the cold, unfamiliar stillness,
we shiver-grope-sigh-struggle-
writhe-despair-wither-and-dry:
until, like March-brown leaves,
we are danced and swirled and whisked
across the unconcerned road
without making a sound

light fails; night falls

light fails—
    something i ought to remember
    sometime before the creation of dawn

faded ribbons of pastel
retreat into thunderous dusk
forcing away the day

light fails—
    something left unsaid
    someone left somewhere
    somehow left undone

cruel reminders
    of day's remainders
awaken me into up

and then . . .

night falls—

misty mystery

during the blur
  of misty morning light,
a recollection
  of the previous night's
  motions and emotions
  came after me,
  prompting reappraisal:

while, after you,
  I found myself forced
  to erase and rephrase
  one who had entered me
  after I, you—

then, the reflection
  clarified itself
  in the mirror
  which stared back
  as a face
  punctuated with sleepless eyes,
  framed by Mab-disheveled hair;

the dreamless visage
  smiled mysteriously at me
  as I thought of you
  thinking of me
  thinking of you
  and
  as I imagined
  kneeling happily at your feet,
  drowning dizzily in your love

Moondog,

you pedal proudly
through streets indifferent,
flags fluttering your presence
in the Fantasy in Lights Parade,
at the Italian Festival,
near the Sixteenth Street Convenient—
vigilantly keeping watch
over this, your city,
as if a younger sibling;
florescent orange vest
spelling out your pseudonym—
a remembrance to gawkers.

but who is it you seek
beyond that cow-eyed stare?
who knows where you live?
who knows your given name?
who sees into who you are?
is it the blind man Lou
who guards the concession stand
in the lobby of the City-County Building
where you usually loiter—
your home away from Grandview Manor?

and then one day someone will, I guess,
wonder aloud about where you have gone
and in silence regret your absence
with belated compassion only

inaction: bicycle without rider

moonset

the muffled moon twists
into horizontal wisps of pastel:
announcing to nocturnal worriers
disheveled daydreams broken by light
as a newspaper thumps the door

natural paradox

the withered mystery:

the final dogwood blossom
pelted into submission by the storm:

its beauty fell earthward,
where it lay against the green
cupping the fresh droplets
until the sun returned

nexus to nothingness

my soul s t r e t c   h   e   s

silently,

blown translucent-white,

like a soap bubble,

floating up—champagney—

up beyond up,   g

                        n

b   u   r   s   t   i

me

into expectation!

out of bounds

i remember that
you sat ensconced
in your recliner,
over-stuffed,
martini spilling
onto pasta-stained sweatshirt;
both of us disencumbered:
you, embarrassed
to be caught lying;
i, embarrassed
for your embarrassment
and my complicitousness—
fumbling to recover
an explanation and
dripping drops
of Old Bombay,
we pretended that
neither noticed
as Tomczak
was picked-off
in the red-zone,
once again, and
we both shouted
the very same vulgarity
simultaneously
to everyone not present
as Frank Gifford
began to dissect
the instant replay

rumor-mongers
(after Alan Dugan)

Christian-cast stones have stayed
yet another seagull from his appointment
with the horizon; broken-winged,
his flash of feathered-flesh fell
to decorate the sandy surface, spread
in imitation of crucifixion—
dirt-made-flesh must so suffer!

like maggots to the rancid, rotting
remains of last week's rubbish,
rumors cling to his festered flesh,
crawling while feeding with slow purpose,
not upon corpus delicti, but upon
life forgotten—rotten, purulent

putrefaction provides invitation to
a host of the pompous enemies of peace
and blue-green shit-flies, one of which
fiddles its hind legs, Nero-like, in the
silent symphony of stench, and the
parasitic assemblage conjugal-dance in
celebration of another's agony, and
meant-to-be-heard whisper-prayers,
sizzling like frying bacon, splatter over
them in an anointment of fatty-oil

the black-massers' exorcism nearly complete:
the incest of dust and fire extinguished
as they await requital; eyes, animal
with arrogance, lifted skyward, the night-
predator steals their defunct sacrifice—the
rising-tide of merciful ocean devours
the carcass; yet, they remain ever-
convinced, ever-vigilant, entrenched
in the muck of the shore—the land
where they reign as lords over them-
selves, the land where the yellow
chrysanthemums bloom underground
in testimony of their very own fates!

self-re-cognition

during those moments
when i notice myself
listening to my own voice,

i wonder inside silently
how deeply he hides within—
he who makes the words for me